Your First

KOI

CONTENTS

Front cover painting by:
D A Lish

Photos by:
Dick Mills,
Frank Naylor,
David Twigg,
David Alderton

©1999 by Kingdom Books PO9 5TL ENGLAND

INTRODUCTION

When you see Koi gliding sedately around their pool, it is quite obvious why they are so popular and attract so much attention. Their intricately-patterned bodies, with brilliant colours blended together or even a single colour with spectacular scalation, are shown to the best effect when seen from above. In this respect, therefore, the Koi is not a fish designed for the aquarium; this fact is emphasised further when you realise that Mother Nature has also designed into the Koi another important component – size. A Koi can grow quite large, often in excess of 75cm (30in) with a girth to match, so suitably-sized living quarters are not going to be of modest proportions.

It is not possible in this small book to detail everything that is needed and should be done to achieve success with keeping Koi – I suggest you read other books for more detailed information. The most important thing to realise is that Koi are not 'just like Goldfish, only bigger'; they come with their own particular requirements, which must be taken into consideration if you are to enjoy all that these fish have to offer.

Although Koi are capable of high-speed swimming, they spend most of their time lazing near the surface.

History

As with the long-established Goldfish, today's Koi has its origins in the Far East where, like many members of the Carp family, it was kept for food. Amongst most animals kept primarily for the larder, there are always a few which seem to appeal more to their owners' aesthetic tastes than to their dietary needs, and these soon become isolated and protected as the family pets. In the case of Koi, perhaps what set some apart was their colouration and, once saved from their original destiny, they were kept separately in their own pool.

Selective breeding has resulted in the cultivated fish we recognise today as Koi. This did not happen overnight or even in the space of a few years, although by some standards the Koi is a very modern fish indeed. There were two

The Kohaku first appeared in Japan in the early 1880s, and is still highly-regarded there today.

important factors in the development of the original Koi – the weather and an imported fish.

In the Niigata province of Japan, winters are long and hard and, to supplement their diet of rice, farmers introduced Carp into the flooded paddy fields. When the ponds were under considerable depths of snow, it is thought that colour pigment changes affected the fish, producing more colourful specimens. Soon the rice farmers began to breed new varieties of these fish. Meanwhile in Europe, particularly in Germany, a variety of Carp had been developed which had far fewer scales, much to the delight of the housewife who up to then had found removing the scales an arduous task. Once live specimens of these fish began to arrive in Japan, they were bred with the native coloured varieties, which produced even more variants in colour, scalation and skin forms. The Koi had arrived. This sequence of events is reported to have taken place from about 1848–1904. Since then, thanks to high-speed air transport, Koi have travelled the world and are now bred in America and Israel as well as in their original home in Japan.

The name 'Koi' is derived from the word 'nishikigoi'. 'Nishiki' may be roughly taken to mean 'brocaded' in the multi-colour sense (referring to the cloth used by well-to-do people) whilst 'koi' is a corruption of 'goi', the word for fish. The scientific name for Koi is Cyprinus carpio. Just to give you an idea of how the different varieties of Koi got their names, the fish developed in Germany passed its name on to the variety of Koi called Doitsu, which is the Japanese word for Germany.

A superb, prize-winning Sanke showing its strong colouration and beautiful patterning.

AQUARIUM OR POND

A hint has already been given as to the unsuitability of Koi for the aquarium and here are more reasons why it is better to keep this particular fish in an outside pond.

Given an adequate diet, Koi grow quickly and need room if they are to develop the correct body shape for their species. In addition to 'horizontal' space, or open areas for swimming, a certain amount of 'vertical' space, or water depth, is also recommended. Moving between the depths as well as swimming horizontally helps to build up the Koi's muscles. This amount of space is better provided out of doors in a garden pond.

Although Koi are available as small (10cm/4in) fish which can be kept in a reasonably-sized aquarium apparently quite happily, you will not be able to keep many of them in such quarters – maybe two or three in an aquarium 30–40cm (12–16in) deep by 90–120cm (3–4ft) long. This figure is a recommended total stocking figure for an aquarium of this size, so immediately the Koi start to grow you are facing problems.

Oxygen levels in the water are only maintained by oxygen coming from the atmosphere at the water's surface, so it follows that the larger this water surface area is, the better. Coldwater aquariums, when stocked with fish that consume oxygen at a fast rate, soon run out of this essential gas, especially on warm days.

Another factor to take into consideration is that Koi have hearty appetites and consume a great deal of food. This must be provided by the fishkeeper or the fish will turn their attention to anything else in the aquarium that they consider to be edible, including aquatic plants. This prodigious appetite has another side effect: a great deal of waste is produced, which has to be dealt with. This calls for a very efficient filtration system if the fish are not to be stressed by having to live in an ever-increasing waste-pit.

Koi make good use of their barbels (the whisker-like growth at each corner of the mouth) to forage about in the gravel bed for food; this action churns up the water and the suspended detritus makes the water cloudy, again requiring a good filter to maintain its clarity. It is true that all these problems will occur in an outdoor pond, but its very much larger water surface area will prevent oxygen depletion whilst the build-up of wastes (should they occur) will form a less significant proportion of the whole volume of water. The pond water will also be reasonably cleaned by the action of wind and rain, but filtration will also be required, and this aspect is covered later.

Finally, it is fair to say that the vast majority of Koi are kept outdoors where their beauty complements the rest of a suitably-designed water garden; it would hardly be practical to keep lifting up the lid of the aquarium (even a big one) just to see the patterns and colours of your Koi.

THE KOI POND

When thinking about putting Koi into a garden pond, you cannot use just any pond. Koi cannot simply be installed into a pond previously stocked with, say, Goldfish. The pond's proportions must be right for their needs.

Pond Dimensions

Within some area of the Koi pond, the water depth should be at least 1.5m (4ft 6in); the pond walls can be almost vertical but there should be shallow areas into which the fish venture for feeding and spawning. By having a deep area in the pond, you will provide the fish with a relatively warm place in which to shelter and rest during the colder part of the year.

The most important dimension of any pond (whether intended for Koi or not) is the area of water exposed to the air. It is here that the pond 'breathes' – ideally, taking in oxygen and emitting carbon dioxide. Despite having a relatively large volume of water, a deep pond also needs to be balanced by having an adequate water surface area: to give some idea of its proportion, if your Koi pond has a surface area of about 6 sq m (approximately 64 sq ft), approximate proportions would be 2 x 3m (6 x 10ft) with a water volume of about 7500 litres (1650 gallons).

Landscape your Koi pond with waterfalls and plants.

This means that you should be able to stock about six fish of a reasonable size. However, there is no hard and fast rule as to the maximum stocking level, as it all depends on the level of the 'life support' systems that you install, and how well you maintain them. Also, what constitutes a 'reasonable size' can be difficult to assess. Whilst Koi can grow to 100cm (30in), most owners are quite happy for them to stop growing when they are about 45–60cm (18–24in). The physical dimensions of the pond also have a limiting effect on the size of the fish.

Construction

Depending on soil type, the pond can be of concrete or a liner type (pre-formed ponds tend to be a little on the small side). Where there is any risk of soil subsidence, then you should avoid concrete. On balance, a hole dug to the required size and lined with a good quality liner (go for the best you can afford) should be adequate. It is not usual to put any material such as gravel or soil on the bottom of the pond for reasons that are explained later.

Design

Make the pond reasonably simple, bearing in mind that any complicated curves in its outline will make it difficult to hide the overlapping wrinkles in the liner. The edges of the liner should reach a little way beyond the edge of the pond and can easily be hidden beneath concrete paving slabs or simply tucked underneath lifted turf surrounding the pond.

Raised ponds are safe

This raised pool will have bottom drains to take the water to the filter.

A simple shape is easier to maintain.

On the one hand, your Koi pond can be a simple fish-holding device, or you can go to the opposite extreme by making it part of a Japanese garden complete with stone lanterns, pagodas and shingle pathways.

A pergola will help to shade the pond without overpowering it.

Siting The Pond

As with all ponds, trees are a major problem so make sure you do not put the pond where it is surrounded by trees. Trees have several drawbacks. Firstly, their roots, if not causing physical obstructions during the pond's installation, may grow longer and stronger and penetrate the liner at a future date. Then there are the problems of leaf-drop in the autumn which may pollute the pond water, and sunshine being blocked from the pond. Whilst too much sunshine can be equally bad, some temporary (or at least controllable) shading can be erected should it become necessary. A pergola, which can be covered either with netting or with attractive climbing shrubs, is one practical solution to shading the pond.

A nearby hedge or fence will shelter the pond from winds and help to cut down on losses from evaporation. From a security aspect, it is important to hide the pond from the gaze of herons, another function that shrubs, hedges or fences can fulfil.

THE 'NON-GREEN' POND

As stated earlier, would-be Koi keepers often believe, wrongly, that these fish can be kept in exactly the same way and conditions as other pond fish. Already, we have discovered that this is not so for a variety of reasons.

Another example of the difference between keeping Koi and other fish is water plants. A planted pond does not simply make the pond more attractive to look at. From the fishkeeper's point of view, plants provide sheltering places and spawning sites for the fish. However, a far more important function provided by aquatic plants is their water-cleaning properties, by removing carbon dioxide and providing surplus oxygen during the process of photosynthesis, and the take-up of nitrates and other nutrients from the water.

As Koi generally look upon most plants as food, or something to displace as they forage, it follows that in a Koi pond these natural water-cleansing agents are at minimum levels. The most obvious indication of this lack of water purification occurs during the warmer weather, when the water in the pond turns bright green and becomes opaque. The reason for this is that during the cold months debris, uneaten food and any decaying vegetation from fallen leaves have been broken down into useful nutrients which simple, one-celled plants use as food once warmth and sunlight return to the pond. These 'mini-plants' are known as algae and they multiply with such speed that their collective presence in the water soon makes it resemble a thick, green soup, universally called 'green water'.

Clearing The Water

Because the cause of green water is due to microscopic celled plants, physical removal by mechanical filtration is difficult – if a dense-enough filter medium could be found to trap the algae, the chances are that it would be too dense for water to flow through it. Normal filtration sponge or open-foam materials are treated by green water simply as though they are not there. Another way to remove the algae has to be found.

A simple method is to use algicides – materials that can be added to the pond water to kill off the algae. These range from 'aquatic weedkillers' to chemical dyes which cut out the light to the pond, thus denying the algae one of its primary needs for survival. All these may do the job of killing the algae, but a side-effect of such treatment is that the mass of dead and subsequently decaying algae consumes much of the oxygen in the water, causing the fish some distress.

Green water can be cleared by using an ultra-violet lamp in conjunction with a mechanical filtration system. Water from the pond is passed by the lamp and ultra-violet rays cause the algae to clump together in lumps large enough for the filter medium to extract them more easily from the water.

The efficiency of algae removal relies on the efficiency of the ultra-violet lamp; its quartz glass surrounding jacket (where fitted) needs to be cleaned regularly so that dirt does not build up on the glass to impair the light from reaching the algae cells as they pass by. Bear in mind that such lamps have a limited life and it is generally

An external filtration system with fitted Ultra-Violet (UV) lamp

recommended that they are replaced each year. Not all ultra-violet lamps need to be fitted directly to an exterior filtration system: one type can be submerged actually in the pond.

Interpet Submersible Uitra-Violet (UV) filter

Blanketweed

Just as algae is the result of excessive nutrients and light in the pond, blanketweed is more likely to appear once you have solved the green water problem. Once the water is returned to a desirable crystal-clear condition, more sunlight can penetrate further into the pond and blanketweed generally soon develops. The not-so-good news is that, although Koi have prodigious appetites, somehow this does not include blanketweed! Although it may appear that the fish are browsing on the weed, it is more likely that they are seeking small aquatic life that hides amongst the green fronds.

There have been many remedies offered for the control or removal of blanketweed, ranging from algicides to barley straw immersed in the pond, as well as an array of magnetic treatments and special substances added to the water which affect the conditions on which blanketweed survival depends.

Blanketweed affects all ponds, not just those containing Koi. In practice, most fishkeepers advocate removing it regularly by hand

Developing Blanketweed

from the moment it first makes an appearance. Use a twisted stick to 'twirl' it out of the water. The one advantage of blanketweed is that it makes excellent compost or mulch for the garden – if your Koi do not want it, at least there is no reason why you shouldn't make use of it elsewhere.

Foaming on the pond surface is due to excess protein caused by over-feeding, over-stocking, the filter not coping with the demand put on it or a build-up of sludge on the bottom of the pond.

Koi are healthy, vigorous fish and we would not want them any other way, but they are also hearty eaters, a characteristic which has one or two slight disadvantages when it comes to keeping the pond clean.

A large intake of food also means a proportionate amount of waste materials being produced. Koi are by nature foraging fish and spend a lot of time searching the pond floor for things to eat. If the pond floor was covered by gravel or soil this would be in a permanent state of disruption with the result that the water would be cloudy. To get the most enjoyment from your Koi, you want to be able to see them at all times; keeping the water clear is a priority, and this means filtration.

There are many forms of filtration systems for ponds (and Koi ponds seem to attract all the variations going). You may want to consider this aspect of the

Because Koi are susceptible to poor water quality, an efficient filtration system is essential. A vast range of equipment is available to achieve this.

pond's management – and how you're going to deal with it – ahead of initial installation. Basically, some system needs to be devised where water is taken from the pond, cleaned, and then returned.

For the smaller Koi pond, an external box filter system is adequate, provided that regular filter maintenance is carried out. In this instance, water is pumped from the pond by a submersible pump in the pond to a filter box which contains cleaning media – brushes and foam blocks for the 'mechanical' straining out of debris and also some form of bacterial-colonising medium to provide 'biological' cleansing of the water to convert otherwise toxic waste materials into less harmful substances.

On a grander scale, some Koi ponds have filtration systems sunk into the ground alongside the main pond; here, water is transferred into the filtration chambers (settlement chambers, followed by brush, foam and biological chambers as before) through horizontal pipes set through the pond's walls. After cleaning has taken place the cleaned water is pumped back into the pond by either a submersible pump set into the final chamber of the in-ground filter or by a 'surface pump' which operates in a dry chamber connected to the filter by a supply pipe.

Hiding The Hardware
If you have gone to a lot of trouble designing your pond to blend in with its surroundings, you do not want the filtration units to spoil the picture. Fortunately, the external box-type filters are easily hidden in the shrubbery or rockery next to the pond whilst the in-ground type can have attractive wooden decking placed over it to form a patio (remember that you need access to both types of filter for regular maintenance).

Aeration
The continuous supply of oxygen to the pond is vital and one bonus of having a filtration system is that it keeps the water 'on the move'. Any disturbance of the water surface is beneficial in this respect as it not only allows oxygen to enter more easily but also helps to disperse unwanted carbon dioxide. The need for oxygen is particularly important during warm months and at these times the water (already depleted of oxygen) returning from the filter can be fed through device called a venturi (available from aquatic shops), which helps to draw extra air into the pond, thus providing the much-needed aeration.

If you haven't got a venturi, and you find the fish are gasping for air at the surface on hot nights, you can alleviate their condition by turning on the fountain or allowing a hose to trickle fresh water through the pond whilst the warm conditions last.

Waterfalls help to produce the much needed oxygen the pond needs during warm months.

By now, it should be obvious that there is absolutely no difficulty in feeding Koi; in fact, it seems the only likely problem is keeping up with their voracious demands.

Koi have a continuous digestive system, with no stomach as such. Like all Carp, they are constant feeders. This means that they appear to take in food whenever it is offered but, if they are over-fed, much of the food could pass straight through undigested, to emerge as a potential water pollutant.

One of the highlights of keeping fish is watching them eagerly eat their food. Always use a good quality food and never be tempted to use the cheaper trout pellets.

As regards food content, the Koi diet should contain carbohydrates, and such diets are extremely well provided by the commercial manufacturers of Koi foods. In addition, the food should also include stabilised Vitamin C and Spirulina to help the fish maintain a natural resistance against disease and to enhance their colours. The composition of the food varies according to both the age of the fish and the season of the year.

A young fish obviously has much more growing to do than an adult, so its diet can contain more protein during the developing stage. As water temperatures cool, digestion becomes impaired, so during early spring and later in autumn it is advisable to feed a more easily-digested diet. An excellent way of doing this is to change over gradually to a diet containing more wheatgerm as water temperatures fall; then, as the fish emerge from their winter resting period, give wheatgerm-based foods before changing up to a fuller diet for the warmer months.

You will be rewarded for your care by happy, healthy Koi.

Types Of Food

As it is in the interests of the Koi-keeper to know exactly how much food the fish are taking, both for the reason stated above and to save money, the use of floating foods is recommended. The food remains visible for long periods so it is easier to judge the amount eaten; if faster-sinking food is given, the length of time it spends on the pond floor cannot be assessed accurately. All foods produced for Koi contain the vital nutrients and vitamins but it is a good idea to vary the 'brand names' from time to time as the exact mixture of ingredients varies between products. As well as the 'basic staple diet' mixture there are other foods produced to enhance the colours.

There are foods other than those produced commercially for Koi which the fish will take with relish. Fishkeepers will know about the benefits of the common earthworm and of providing live foods such as Daphnia, Bloodworm and perhaps well-cleaned Tubifex; pieces of brown bread are also snapped up quickly as are prawns and lettuce. Don't forget that Koi will also supplement the food you provide with whatever else they can find in the pond during the warmer months when aquatic life (insects, frog-spawn, tadpoles) and soft-leaved plants are well established.

How To Feed

It should come as no surprise that Koi, because of their appetite and constant quest for food, visit the area of the pond where the food is regularly given and consequently become hand-tame. Here you should exercise caution and, for the reasons stated above, not feed them every time they rise to greet you.

Feeding twice a day should be quite adequate, but the amount can be increased as the fish grow. Feeding at the same part of the pond not only gets the fish used to where the food is provided but ensures that they gather there, so providing you with an ideal opportunity to check them over as they feed.

At each feed, give enough food for the fish to clear up in approximately five minutes – this will satisfy the fish but not pollute the pond.

As your Koi become more used to you and start to recognise a regular routine, you may be able to train them to feed from your hand.

BUYING

At this stage, as a newcomer to Koi-keeping, probably you will be buying Koi for the most basic of reasons and by using the most basic method: you want a Koi and will buy the one you most like the look of. However, matters can be more complicated for more experienced Koi-keepers, when the reasons for their choice involve the particular aspect of Koi-keeping they are concerned with (keeping for pleasure, exhibiting or breeding), and cause a whole new set of parameters to come into play. In this book, we will consider what to look for in general terms.

Where To Buy

Always go to a reputable Koi dealer or to an established Koi keeper when buying your fish. It may also be prudent to buy Koi within your local area rather than at a more distantly-located Koi show. The reason for this is twofold: firstly, it will avoid stressing the new fish by introducing it into a very different set of water conditions from those it is used to; secondly, transporting the new fish for a long distance causes another form of stress that it is best to avoid.

When To Buy

Whilst imports of Koi usually occur in the autumn, after the stock collection from breeders' ponds, it is probably better for the novice fishkeeper to buy in the spring so that the fish can be acclimatised (and the fishkeeper's experience built up) during the warmer months before the next winter has to be faced.

What To Look For

Koi are displayed in ponds and you should spend some time looking at the whole scene before selecting your fish. Check out the condition of the pond – is the water clean and does it smell healthy? Are all the fish active and do they seem to be seeking attention? The answers to these two questions should assure you that the fish are fit and healthy at least.

Turning to the fish themselves, disregard any that have obvious visible defects such as deformities, spots, bumps, lumps and poor colour. (On second thoughts, if they display these signs of poor quality, it might be better to go elsewhere.)

The fish's skin should have a lustrous look to it with the colour patterning clearly defined. The fish should be able to swim and maintain its chosen position in the water without effort. All this can be ascertained from a distance but to inspect the fish more closely ask the dealer to capture it in a large bowl or perforated crate and bring it to the pondside for you. Here you can look at all its physical aspects – clear eyes, belly not swollen or shrunken, no damage to fins, and so on.

Right: When buying young Koi, you must realise that their markings will probably change as they grow. As this Sanke ages, more red or black colouring may appear.

Bringing Koi Home

The fish should be placed in a large elongated plastic bag with sufficient water to cover its dorsal fin; depending on the length of journey time, extra oxygen may be added. A second bag is usually placed over the first as extra security and then the whole thing is placed in a darkened bag or cardboard box.

If you are travelling by car, place the Koi across the boot. If you place it 'fore and aft', each time the car brakes or accelerates the fish bangs its nose or tail against the ends of the bag, whereas when placed 'across ways' the fish only suffers a sideways roll or two.

Home At Last

The question of quarantine is hotly debated; whilst seemingly a good thing, many keepers argue that it is yet another unnecessary stress for the fish. Then you have to consider the necessity of providing good quality water and living space for the fish whilst it is in quarantine. One observation that defies argument is that when buying your very first collection of fish (not the full complement that the pond can hold at one time, please) any 'quarantining' can take place in the pond as there are no other fish to become contaminated.

The fish should be floated, still in its transportation bag, in the pond for a period of time to allow the two water temperatures to equalise, after which it can be released into the pond. Don't expect the fish to rise up and greet you immediately; it will take a few days for it to get used to its new surroundings.

When choosing Koi, the fish should be placed in an inspection bowl so that you can look at them closely.

VARIETIES

To the newcomer, the tongue-twisting Japanese names seem to be an unsurmountable hurdle and, indeed, the prospect of telling the difference between a Showa-Sanke from a Taisho-Sanke is not helped by the fact that the former is described as having red and black markings on a white body as against red and white markings on a black body! Similarly, there are different words used for apparently the same colour. Take, for instance, the colour red: this can be described with the word 'Aka' when it is a background hue whilst 'Hi' is used for a pattern or foreground colour.

Koi come in a range of colours with a variety of names.

Names Of Koi Colours Colour Strains

Ai: blue
Midori: green
Aka: red as background
Newzu: grey
Orenji: orange
Cha: brown
Shiro: white

Karasu: black as a background
Gin: silver
Ki: yellow
Sumi: black (as markings)
Kin: gold

Hi: red (as pattern or foreground)
Beni: orange-red (as background)

Thanks to intensive breeding programmes over the years, many colour strains of Koi have become fixed and are recognised the world over – single-coloured and multi-coloured fish all vie for attention in the dealers' pools.

The visual attraction of Koi is not limited to simply the colours alone for these are complemented by the patterns that they form; in addition, there are extra physical details to be found in the scalation (or lack of it). Scales can be arranged in simple patterns, have dark centres, shiny metallic lustres and even, taking in today's craze for dramatic effect, be transplanted to form designs on the fish's flanks.

Popular Varieties

The following are some of the popular varieties of Koi which you will see without too much trouble whenever you go to a dealer or to a Koi show.

The Ogon (pronounced *Oh-gone)* is a single-coloured Koi, usually silver or gold. These fish can make a sharp contrast in the pond when kept with other highly-patterned Koi.

White Koi with markings:
Kohaku, Tancho Kohaku, Koromo, Shiro Bekko
Three-coloured Koi:
Showa Sanke, Taisho Sanke
Metallic Koi:
Ogon, Gin Matsuba, Kin Matsuba
Black Koi with other colours:
Hi Utsuri, Ki Utsuri
Blue Koi:
Asagi, Shusui

Showa Sanke

Shiro Bekko

Kawarimono

Tancho Sanke

BREEDING

Although you may be at the very beginning of your Koi-keeping career, you will be pleased to know that they breed quite easily in the pond. All that is needed is a length of time for them to mature, to be kept in the best of conditions and fed quality food. That's the theory, anyway, for the production of good quality Koi depends on many other things.

Despite their individual, often spectacular colours and markings, when it comes to breeding Koi are no respecters of either of these. They will interbreed without a moment's thought and this poses a problem for the Koi breeder in much the same way as for other animal breeders – keeping the strain pure. (Is there an equivalent term for a mongrel Koi, the result of an unplanned breeding?)

Female Koi ready for breeding can be recognised by their deeper bodies and more obvious roundness in the body, especially when viewed from above. Males generally have slimmer bodies overall but may develop slightly longer and more pointed pectoral fins; additionally, the male's gill covers and pectoral fin rays carry small white spots called 'tubercles', but do not regard these as being visible symptoms of White Spot Disease!

Spawning will occur spontaneously irrespective of the markings of the fish, so if you want to raise certain strains of Koi both parents should have the same characteristics; segregating the fish (by variety or by sex) into separate ponds will help to minimise production of 'mongrel' fish.

How Koi Breed

Like Goldfish, Koi are egglaying fish which means that the female expels eggs from her body at the precise moment that the male expels sperm from his. The eggs and sperm mix in the pond water and the eggs become fertilised to hatch independently of any further action by the adult fish.

It is necessary to protect the eggs from the fish as they represent a tasty meal. For this reason, spawning barriers are used. These long, stiff bristled brushes or mats are draped across the water surface into which the male drives the female when spawning. The expelled and fertilised eggs lodge in the brushes whose stiffness deters the fish from following.

Eggs hatch in a matter of days but they can be collected from the brushes immediately after spawning and placed in a separate aquarium or small pond to hatch; alternatively, the whole spawning brush or mat can be lifted out and transferred, complete with fertilised eggs, to another pond for hatching.

Selecting The Parent Fish

Because Koi are such easy breeders, it is quite simple to breed from fish chosen for their physical characteristics and kept separately from each other until they are ready to spawn. A further method is for the fish never to meet at all – eggs are stripped from the female by hand and mixed in water with sperm similarly collected from the chosen male. In either instance, the outcome of the spawning is reasonably predictable with a high proportion of the offspring showing the desired characteristics.

This is a deliberately over-simplified account of a highly skilled business, perfected by Koi-keepers over many years, which should not be attempted by the novice breeder.

Raising The Young Fish

Following the absorption of the nutrient-filled yolk-sac a few days after hatching, the young Koi can be fed on commercially-available fry foods, brine shrimp and sifted Daphnia in much the same way that Goldfish fry are dealt with.   As the fish grow, not only should they be given more (and bigger) food but they will require extra space. Also you do need to sort out the young and get rid of those you do not want in order to keep only the desired strains of good fish.

The wide body of this Sanke tells us that it is a female. Males tend to be thinner and more torpedo-shaped.

HEALTH

The health of any fish kept in captivity depends entirely on the quality of its environment and care. Unlike the fish in nature, the captive fish cannot swim away either in search of more food or from poor conditions – they have to endure what is provided by their owner. By giving them good water conditions and a carefully-controlled diet, you have done your part to ensure that the fish have built up their natural immunity against disease and are less likely to contract any illness through stress brought on by bad pond management. However, there are occasions when things do go wrong and your fish appears to be less than at its best.

The best form of diagnosis needs only a good 'eye' coupled with understanding cause and effect. The best starting point is to 'know your fish', that is, to recognise what is their normal appearance and behaviour; anything then not quite normal becomes instantly apparent. Most easily-visible external symptoms mean that any problem will be non-fatal and able to be treated successfully. It is only where something is 'going on inside' that the illness turns out to be more difficult to treat successfully as, by the time exterior signs are seen, it is usually too late to save the fish.

There are generally two methods of treating a sick fish: individually or collectively. When treated individually, medication is administered in a separate 'hospital' aquarium or pond; collectively, the whole of the main pond is treated. In either instance, the exact amount of water volume in both aquarium or pond needs to be known if accurate dosing of medication is to be made. Always use medications specifically made not only to cure the problem in question but also one formulated especially for use with Koi. Most of the following problems can be dealt with by the new Koi keeper without too much trouble. Other illnesses, which include dropsy and tuberculosis, may require expert diagnosis and treatment, and veterinary or expert Koi help should be sought.

Signs To Look For

General listlessness, failing to rise for food, repeatedly 'flicking' the body against objects in the pond, fading colours, gasping at the surface, spots and fungal growths are all symptoms that may be seen at some time – hopefully not all at once!

Flicking, or 'flashing' as it is also described, may be due to irritating skin parasites; if further parasites attack the gills, then the absorption of oxygen may be affected and the fish gasps at the surface even though there may be plenty of oxygen in the water. Parasites may be removed physically or by treating the water with the relevant remedy. Listlessness and fading colours may reflect poor water quality – the filter may need cleaning, or there may be a high level of toxic material in the water. Spots (usually small white ones) might be regarded as the fish equivalent of our common cold – it is fairly common and easily curable with the correct remedy.

Outbreaks of larger spots or even fungus covering the mouth or body can again be treated with easily-available preparations. Fin-rot sounds an awful problem but it is classed as a secondary disease as it tends to occur as a result of poor water quality when bacteria get into a split fin and progress much more swiftly than they would have done under cleaner pond conditions.

Because Koi spend some time cruising just beneath the water surface, they can be prone to attack from predators such as herons and cats. Even if the attack is unsuccessful the fish can be left with deep scratches that need attention. A further result of such an attack is that the fish will become very nervous about venturing up from the bottom and well may hide from view (even when tempted by food) for two or three weeks at a time.

. Like their native relative, the Carp, Koi are long-lived fish and life-spans of well over 20 years are not unknown. With all the excellent care you will be giving your Koi, you will be rewarded for many years to come.

Koi are stunningly beautiful fish, so it comes as no surprise that their proud owners want to show them off to other fishkeepers, and perhaps win some prizes along the way.

Koi shows are very popular throughout the summer months and there are national organisations set up to cater for the exhibition of Koi. The Koi show may be a one-day event (each one organised by a local section of a Koi-keeping Society) or it may cover a whole weekend on a larger scale.

A good sign of a healthy Koi is its erect fins, as on this Sanke. Koi that continuously hold their fins down and against their body could be showing a sign of poor health or poor water quality.

SHOWING

While an aquarium fish which is viewed side-on, each fish in its own show tank, Koi exhibiting is arranged by a different method. To carry a sufficient number of large aquariums so that each Koi can be shown individually is obviously impractical, so Koi are exhibited in show vats, large circular containers resembling deep, portable paddling pools. The fish are placed in these vats and the judges progress from vat to vat judging the fish therein. An important thing to remember is that traditionally Koi are expected to be viewed from above, so vat-viewing is not so difficult or out of the ordinary as might be first assumed.

There are two methods of exhibiting Koi at shows depending on which fish go into each vat. In one case, each Koi-keeper can place all his fish in one vat, regardless of their variety or size, and each fish is then judged on its own merits. With the second method, only fish of the same size and/or variety are put into a vat and these fish may have different owners. Each method has its advocates with probably the only real advantage to the 'non-Koi' expert coming in the second instance as the winner is easily recognisable from amongst single variety/size entries, whereas the award winners from a 'mixed bag' are more difficult to distinguish.

The range of classes for exhibiting Koi is wide, with 'Baby' and 'Mature' being yet two more categories to add to the wide number available for each variety.
There are many Koi Societies throughout the country and around the world. Referring to your local Society will bring more practical information than could ever be included in even the largest Koi book.

An array of Koi vats at a show.

At competitions, Koi are segregated into size classes. This picture depicts
three different size groupings.

KOI SOCIETIES

The majority of locally-based Koi Societies organise annual shows and regular visits to other Koi Society members' ponds. It is not unknown for some societies to organise a trip to Japan so that members can see Koi in their original home – and to bring back fish as well!

Membership secretaries of the major Koi Societies at the time of publication are:

British Koi-keepers Society
Membership Secretary
Pip Ostel
Craig Varr
Beechwood Avenue
Thurmaston
Leicestershire LE4 8HA

Zen Nippon Airinkai
(South of England Chapter)
Tony Price
Montana
Closewood Road
Denmead
Waterlooville
Hants PO7 6JD

North of England Koi Club
Tony McCann
45 May Road
Swinton
Manchester M27 5FS

Mid-Atlantic Koi Club
Anita and Charles Walker
11794 Target Court
Woodbridge
VA 22192
USA

BIBLIOGRAPHY

THE PROFESSIONAL'S BOOK OF KOI
Anmarie Barrie
ISBN 0-86622-528-5
TS-158
A wonderful introduction to the world of Koi, this book discusses everything that Koi need in order to thrive and be healthy.
Hardcover: 250 x 170mm, 160 pages, 150 full colour photographs and drawings.

THE PERFECT POND RECIPE BOOK
Peter J May
ISBN 185279007-5
GB 002
An easy-to-follow pictorial hand-book to help any would-be pond owner avoid the pitfalls and problems associated with pond construction and design.
Hardcover: 250 x 170mm, 32 pages, full colour illustrations throughout.

THE COMPLETELY ILLUSTRATED GUIDE TO KOI FOR YOUR POND
Dr Herbert Axelrod et al
ISBN 0-7938-0597-X
TS-268
This is the ultimate Koi book, covering all varieties from the traditional Japanese to the new Israeli and American modifications. Beautiful as well as immensely thorough, useful and interesting, this is a milestone in Koi literature.
Hardcover: 300 x 225mm, fully illustrated with colour photographs and illustrations.

KOI VARIETIES: JAPANESE COLOURED CARP - NISHIKIGOI
Dr Herbert R Axelrod
ISBN: 0-86622-162-X
PS-875
This colourful book covers the many varieties available, selection and history of Koi. Not only is the development of both the fish and the hobby covered but the Japanese names are also explained. The book is illustrated with over 250 full colour photographs.

A good example of a Tancho Sanke: a nice black and white body with a good, round Tancho red disc on the head.